DISSONANCE - A COLLECTION OF POETRY

ARCHISMAN PAL

Made with ❤ on the Notion Press Platform
www.notionpress.com

Contents

Contents

Contents

Preface

Welcome to my world.

What you are holding in your hand right now is the book equivalent of my mind. All these words, all these verses, they are my way of turning fleeting thoughts into something tangible. Each poem in this collection carries a little piece of me - whether it be from real life, or my imagination. Perhaps you, the reader, will find yourself in these pages. Perhaps you will find them relatable, or they will remind you of your own experiences. If these poems can offer comfort, clarity, or even the feeling of being understood, then they have done their job.

Additionally, I have included a playlist at the end of the book, which are the songs which helped inspire some of the poems in this book.

Thank you!

2nd March,

2025.

Acknowledgements

No book can be created in isolation, and this one is no exception.

My immense thanks goes out to:

My mother, for fostering this fire in me and allowing me to write,

My close friends, for reading, reviewing, and criticising my poetry,

My teachers, for giving me the required guidance and always helping me,

To Gia and Viva Marie, for putting up with me and writing three poems with me.

And finally, thank you to you, the reader, for picking up this book and giving these poems a chance. I hope you enjoy your read!

1. Blankheart

Thought I finally had it,
One chance, just a fraction,
Should've been scientific,

Third law, reaction,
But I was merely the action,
Which I did not get back.
After all this effort,
My heart is still blank.
It isn't right to hope
After all of this,
But I still wish I found it,
And did not miss.

2. About Nostalgia

about nostalgia

"A wistful yearning for the past".
That's the definition of nostalgia.
But should you keep looking back,

Or move on to life's next stanza?
A pleasurable feeling, tinged with sadness,
Is all nostalgia brings to the table.
In reality, it's nothing but a mind's trick,
To get us thinking of our past as a fable.
A nostalgic craving to return to happier times
Might serve as a delightful escape,
But this getaway is not really eternal,
Soon enough, you'll have a lot on your plate.
In conclusion, is nostalgia good or bad?
It helps us, makes us happier and brighter,
But too much gets us stuck on the past,
And makes the present a whole lot darker.

3. Missing 2.0

missing 2.0

Sitting in public, but zoning out,
Wishing you never came.
Saying hi to people around you,

But you can't even remember their name.
Feeling like closing your eyes,
And just fading away.
Feeling more lost than ever before,
More than you could say.
No one to share jokes with,
None of your friends showed up.
Feeling less and less energized with passing time,
Not even wanting to fill your cup.
Feeling alone like never before,
Missing that one best friend,
The one who could show up and
Make all your loneliness end.

4. Mirror

mirror

When I look upon you,
All that I think of is advice.
Things that I could've said to myself,

So that I didn't pay the price.
When I look upon you,
I gaze deep into my thoughts,
Reflected upon my irises,
Hovering over my wrongs.
When I look upon you,
I see all my dreams and joy.
You are a reminder that life goes on,
And that I should enjoy.
When I look upon you,
I see myself, much clearer.
You provide valuable introspection,
For that I thank you, mirror.

5. Out Of Tune

out of tune

Something was wrong, he could sense it,
Yes, it's true that she was leaving,
But the violins were playing out of tune,

As her frame glistened in the light of the moon.
He rushed out after her, into the street,
She stopped, from him barely two feet,
And painfully but determinedly, braced herself
For the goodbye, and the end of themselves.
He saw the tears streaming down her face,
And said, without a moment to waste,
"You're the closest to me, you're my partner-in-crime",
"Everyday, it's like I fall for you for the very first time."
"You are the best thing that's ever been mine",
"Without you, life would lose all its shine."
She smiled, and realized she was fine.
They walked back to their house, their hands intertwined.

6. Two Hearts

Never thought I would, but I met you again,
Walking on the street, as if nothing had changed.
Almost passed you by, but then I caught

That familiar glint in your eyes, still unchained.
I hesitated, the years lost between us
But you recognized me, and smiled without thought,
I found myself smiling back, unsure,
As we talked about the paths we had both sought.
In that very moment, I wondered if
The animosity between us could be laid to rest.
And whether you'd be willing to accept me again,
If I could finally pass all of your tests.
But then you walked away, as if I was
Nothing more than just an old friend.
You said goodbye, and turned your back,
And left me with nothing to mend.
You were a language I was once fluent in,
A language that I still know how to read.
But, maybe forever belongs to memories,
It's never meant for two hearts to succeed.

7. Back Home to You

back home to you

You speak of hope and happiness,
Of skies that clear when storms have passed.
You tell them pain won't last forever,

Although you still linger in the past.
You wrap your words like bandages,
Covering up wounds you cannot see.
A healer's hands, soft and steady,
But never turned to set yourself free.
You whisper, "You are not alone",
While silence surrounds your chest.
You lift them up with quiet strength,
Yet sink beneath your own unrest.
But maybe someday, when you speak,
Your words will reach your heart too.
And all the joy you gave away,
Will finally come back home to you.

8. Diphylleia Grayi

She was like diphylleia grayi.
A fragile blossom, almost out of sight.
With petals white and soft like secrets,

Shy against the morning light.
No one knew her deep and true,
Or her inner persona, hidden so well.
That is, until his rain arrived,
Then, he could clearly tell.
The veil of white faded to glass,
Not broken, not erased, but revealed.
He saw who she was, genuine and authentic,
To her, it was as if she was healed.
Like diphylleia grayi, she turned translucent,
A skeleton flower's soul left bare.
And he swore his rain to be never-ending,
For her, he promised to always care.

9. Sonder

sonder

Whenever I look out my window,
I see a sea of faces, blurred and wide.
Each passing stranger, lost in thought,

Fading like waves in an endless tide.
A woman hums a quiet tune,
Perhaps on her way to a place called home.
While a man walks with weary steps,
Chasing time that's never his own.
A child runs past with laughing eyes,
Oblivious to the world around him.
While an old man sits with a distant gaze,
Recalling days that seem so dim.
The buses groan, the cars rush past,
The world spins on, so vast, so loud.
A thousand stories cross and fade,
Each lost within the faceless crowd.

10. Change

change

A realization like thunder, without warning,
A shift so sudden, sharp, and clear.
Suddenly, everything made complete sense,

And truth stood waiting, always near.
A door once open now swings gently,
Not slammed, not locked, just left behind.
No sudden breaks, no jagged endings,
Just distance growing, undefined.
A dream collapses, thin like paper,
Dissolving with the morning air.
The mind reaches out to hold the edges,
But nothing solid lingers there.
The clock hands meet, the world stands still,
A hush before the night moves on.
And just like that, the moment shatters,
One last breath, and the past is gone.

11. Colors

colors

She used to dream in neon lights,
In golden rays and electric blues,
The world had shimmered, vast and bright,

A canvas fresh with brilliant hues.
But the years had drained the colors out,
Like water on paint, it bled away.
Now everything is black and white,
A muted sky, a washed-out day.
She tries to find the spark again,
To light the dark, to chase the glow.
But every dream feels out of reach,
A fading echo, dim and slow.
Yet somewhere deep in the gray,
A flicker hums, still holding on.
And maybe, if she waits enough,
The colors aren't completely gone.

12. Postcard From the Future

Dear me, be careful.
Things are going to change,
Some for the better, or worse,

Life is becoming really strange.
Dear me, always look up.
Even when the stress is high,
When the darkness surrounds you,
Even when you want to cry.
Dear me, never lose hope.
Keep walking towards your destiny,
The road may twist, and dusk may fall,
But the dawn will come eventually.
Dear me, it will be okay.
Not all battles leave a scar.
Some will break you, some will teach you,
But you have made it this far.

13. Happiness

happiness

You hold joy like a fragile thread,
Afraid it snaps if pulled too tight.
You trace the edges, never trying,

As if it's bound to fade from sight.
Laughter lingers on your lips,
But never settles, never stays.
You keep happiness behind closed doors,
Too scared to let it see the day.
You've seen the sun slip past the hills,
Felt warmth dissolve into bleak cold.
So now you flinch at every sunrise,
Convinced that light won't take hold.
But even waves that leave the shore,
Return to feel the land once more.
And happiness, no matter how fleeting,
Is still a treasure you cannot ignore.

14. Liquid Love

You say your love is like a liquid,
With your heart as its container.
That's the dumb and poetic excuse you gave,

When you revealed yourself as a heartbreaker.
You say your love has a greater volume
Than that of the supposed beaker.
But you have the choice to close pipes,
As if your heart was a controller.
You say the liquid has to go somewhere
After closing off a dysfunctional conduit.
But those pipes must be clogged after exceeding use,
The problem? You just haven't realized it.
You say that there are connections,
But maybe you are the one connecting them all.
You think you have a huge, too-full beaker,
In reality, it just might be empty and small.

15. Imperfect Perfections

imperfect
perfections

She closes her eyes, and there she stands,
Taller, lighter, free of doubt.
A version carved from every wish,

The one she'd swore she'd figure out.
It walks with grace, with quiet ease,
No second-guessing in its stride.
But when it turns to meet her gaze,
She sees the cracks it tries to hide.
Its hands still shake, its breath still halts,
It wears her sorrow like a scar.
Perfection was a trick of light,
Not something built, just something far.
She doesn't run, she takes its hand,
Not to replace, but to befriend.
For being whole was never flawless,
It was learning where to mend.

16. Mathematics

To most, mathematics is probably
Something to hate, a dull routine.
But to people who romanticize,

It feels more like a tragic scene.
Take for example parallel lines.
They share the same fate, side by side.
Their slopes are perfectly aligned,
Yet a meeting is always denied.
Another case would be asymptotes.
They draw so near, yet never touch,
So close to feeling something real,
Yet the gap remains too much.
Saddest of all are the intersecting lines.
They touch for a moment bittersweet,
Then drift away forevermore,
Their paths no more to meet.

17. Poetry

Some moments slip through the cracks,
But linger like a deep dream.
A half-remembered melody,

A whisper, lost in quiet streams.
Some realities are too heavy,
Too raw to rest in open air,
So they linger in quiet hearts,
A weight too deep to share.
Some souls are stitched from stardust,
Restless, drifting, never still.
It is as if the universe forgot,
To teach them how to heal.
And so poets gather fleeting moments,
Truths too heavy, sharp to mourn,
The restless souls that time unwinds,
This is why poetry was born.

18. Mooncycles

mooncycles

There are times we fade to nothing,
Like footprints lost in drifting sands.
Thoughts scattered like dust around the world,

Swept away by fleeting chance.
There are days we feel like mere echoes,
A shadow of what we once were.
Lost in the weight of unspoken thoughts,
As our memories start to blur.
Yet slowly, light seeps through the cracks,
Softly reaching where darkness grew.
Fostering it with happiness and hope,
Turning it into something new.
Like the moon, we wane to crescents,
Dimming, shrinking, just before –
The tides return, the cycle calls,
And we rise to shine once more.

19. Texting Habits

She types, pauses, and hesitates.
A message waiting, half-complete.
A simple "hello" feels far too late,

Too sudden, or too bittersweet.
She wonders what they think of her,
If she's just a fleeting name,
Or if she's just a thought, a blur,
A lost player in a never-ending game.
She writes, deletes, and writes again.
Afraid to seem too curious, too loud.
Would they still welcome her as then,
Or would she just be lost in the crowd?
Her fingers hover, then retreat.
She shakes her head, locks up her phone.
Perhaps it's best to not connect,
Perhaps they're better left alone.

20. Black Hole

black hole

Recently, there's been word of
Stars being emitted from a black hole.
The object meant to symbolize destruction,

Yet somehow, it still lets go.
A mouth that swallows time and light,
But spits out galaxies anew.
A force that can unmake the heavens,
But scatters stars like the morning dew.
Isn't it strange how even endings
Can twist into another start?
How even darkness, vast and endless,
Still holds creation in its heart?
Maybe the end is not so final,
Maybe the dark still yearns to give.
What should consume without a whisper,
Instead lets dying embers live.

21. Above the Snowline

Above the snowline, there's nothing.
Not even a pinch of green,
It's all white and sometimes grey,
But it's still a sight to be seen.

Above the snowline, there's nothing.
No sparks of verdancy.
But what you'll find there, is true, and calm
And free from any controversy.
Above the snowline, there's nothing.
It's just a rocky, snowy place.
But you will find solitary tranquility,
And your inner emotions, you will face.
Above the snowline, there's peace.
Serenity surrounded by snowflakes,
Just the feeling of being on top of the world,
Is enough to put on your life some brakes.
I heard that above the snowline there's nothing,
It's all barren, devoid of life's embrace.
But when I went up there, I found my solace,
A paradoxical heaven, a sacred space.

22. Book of Love

He loved her like a story told
Careful and soft, page by page.
Every chapter built from longing,

Written in ink that would never fade.
But she was wind, not steady hands,
Turning pages, then she left.
Closing the book without warning,
Leaving the ending second-guessed.
But she left behind a poet's curse,
A love that lingers, ink-stained deep.
He writes her name in every shadow,
Forever a ghost that he has to keep.
He does not mourn, he does not plead,
His wounds turn to endless rhymes.
For poets do not cry for love,
They only bleed between the lines.

23. Day & Night

day & night

with Viva Marie

Sunlight peeks through the open door,
Lighting the room in a golden glow.

He was like the day, in every way,
The summer sun, an amber ray.
And there she sat, in shadows deep.
A winter's frost, she chose to keep.
The golden light brushed pale, cold skin,
But failed to thaw the ice within.
He reached for her with an open flame,
His warmth calling out her icy name,
But to her, it felt too bright,
A stark contrast against her silent night.
She shied away from his blazing touch,
Her soul too cold, to feel too much.
She liked her dark, her winter, her night,
And she wished that he understood her fright.
He loved her true, like a fiery blaze,
But it ran wild, and chased her away.
She loved him too, but in a different light,
Like the glow of the moon, just out of sight.
And when he felt the way he did,
He couldn't help but let it show.
But she closed off and hid from him,
Her touch ice cold, like winter snow.
And so, sunlight peeks through the door,
Lighting the room in a golden glow.
And though she tried to lock it and stay far,
The summer breeze pushes it ajar.
He was like the day, in every way.
The summer sun, an amber ray.
A winter tundra, a sunny bay,

And maybe, maybe someday,
They would come to the fall.
He could stand to cool,
And she could stand to lose
And the day & night could stand at a truce.

24. Garden Below

The garden rang with laughter,
As the morning sun bathed the leaves,
The children ran, their voices high,

Their joy entwined with the summer breeze.
The flowers bloomed in endless hues,
Their fragrance drifting through the air,
The trees stood tall with emerald crowns,
Draped in sunlight, radiant and fair.
He stood apart, and watched them play.
So full of life, with hearts aglow,
His eyes strayed to the tallest tree of all,
And wondered if they'd ever know.
For beneath the tree's embracing shade,
A grave lay hidden, calm and deep.
Yet all of this was once a wish,
A dream that he had sworn to keep.

25. Echoes

He was walking through his old room,
Trying to organize all his antiques.
When his eyes found a hidden box,

And decided to give it a curious peek.
On opening it, he saw a bunch of paper,
Some even yellowing at the edges.
His fingers brushed over the fragile sheets,
With ink fading like lost, forgotten pledges.
As he read the words, his memory stirred,
His mind found stories from long ago.
Tales of memories, almost obscured from view,
Containing life's anecdotes, with knowledge aglow.
With every letter, he felt time collapse,
The threads of his family weaving through space,
Records of their journeys, humble but grand,
Filling him with peace, a soothing embrace.
Every blot of ink, a heartbeat of the past.
Each one a reminder of lives they led.
He decided to write his own chapter right then,
To pen his own lines in the family thread.

26. Dandelions

dandelions

It drifted past the hills and streams,
A silver ghost in the golden light.
No tether bound, no path to trace,

just carried soft and out of sight.
It followed the wind throughout the sky,
A fleeting wisp, so light, so small,
No roots to hold, no chains to break,
Just weightless in the air's soft call.
It twirled through the afternoon,
Past reaching hands and laughter bright,
A whispered dream upon the wind,
A brief spark in endless flight.
It never knew where it'd land.
Nor if it'd rest and roam once more,
Yet still it drifted, lost, unbound,
A wanderer forevermore.

27. Clouds

They love me best when I'm painted,
In hues of gold and blushes of pink,
A sky stretching towards the horizon,

An otherwordly beauty, gone in a blink.
But when I hide the stars in silence,
Or when I steal the sun away,
They scowl, blaming me for the dark,
As if I chose to dim the day.
And when I cry, they curse the rain,
As if relief should be refused.
As if the heart should never free its burden,
As if the mind should always be bruised.
They never think of the light I need,
Or if I ache beneath the strain.
Sometimes, I too need to shed my sorrow,
Like them, I too have the right to rain.

28. Untold

I travel through the world all alone,
Solitary with my thoughts, lost in the crowd.
I notice the small wonders of life,

But loneliness lingers, even with people around.
I see the happiness in other people's eyes,
Yet cannot replicate that for myself.
Their laughter sounds like distant skies,
An ethereal melody, trapped upon a shelf.
The world moves on, but I stand still
Frozen in time as stories unfold
I search for life, but miss the thrill,
Lost in the echoes of tales untold.
I chase the dawn, but miss the light,
My dreams, now coated with regret,
For once, I wish that I could fade to ink,
That I was the poem, not the poet.

29. The Sun

She was always there.

A quiet presence, a steady light,

Filling spaces he never noticed,

Yet keeping all his days bright.
She warmed his days, she lit his way,
Yet never once did he see.
He only spoke when she was dim,
And asked her why she couldn't be.
On days she hid, he called her cold.
On days she burned, he turned away.
He never cared, he never looked,
Yet missed her warmth when she turned gray.
He looked at her like she was the sun,
Taken for granted, day by day.
And only in her golden descent,
Did he beg for her to stay.

30. Sweet Sixteen

SWEET
SIXTEEN

Sweet sixteen,
Should i have remembered something?
Transitioning,

Though I don't feel anything.
Now in the latter half
Of my youth, as it seems.
But if that is so,
Then where's my teenage dream?
I guess time is the key,
For providing solace.
Passing moments provide clues,
To dispel this darkness.
Still so much of my journey,
Left to experience and go through,
No use being down now,
When everything's still new.

31. Solitary World

He watched her build a world alone,
With walls so high, unfit to climb,
She wandered halls of her own thoughts,

Lost in rooms she called divine.
he asked, "Don't you feel the weight?"
"The silence, heavy, cold and deep?"
"A life untouched, a lonely heart,"
"Is that the price of peace you keep?"
She met his gaze, but did not flinch,
Her voice a whisper, yet her words rang true.
"I walk alone, but watch the sky,"
"Why trade the stars for someone's view?"
"They shape your ways, they make your chains,"
"You call it love, but lose the way."
"I'd rather live in a world that's mine,"
"Than be a pawn in someone's play."

32. Stargazing

She had always looked up at the stars.
Finding beauty and comfort in each glance.
She always traced the constellations,

As if they were her path, her chance.
She wondered if they knew her name,
Her thoughts, her wishes, and all her dreams.
After all, the night was her sanctuary,
A safe haven from life's fleeting schemes.
Under their glow, she felt a pull.
A distant ache, yet warm, familiar.
As if the stars weren't just far away,
But stitched to her soul, a force peculiar.
She saw it then – she was not alone,
Each soul, with the stars entwined.
She knew that she was not just looking up,
She was meeting pieces of her kind.

33. Self-Love

self-love

He spent all his time in his mind,
Always finding new ways to hate himself.
Everyone told him love begins within,

But to him, it was on a too-high shelf.
He always flinched at his reflection,
A face he swore he could never change.
No kindness ever seemed to reach him,
It felt like joy was out of his range.
Then he met someone who spoke in warmth,
Saw the glow in places he had ignored.
She traced his scars, but still held on,
With his heart, she struck a chord.
She saw his ghosts, but did not flinch,
Held him gently, called them past.
And in her eyes, he saw himself,
Not as fading, but built to last.

34. Tell/Ask

TELL/ASK

Tell me a story,

I will always listen carefully.

After all, I need some color in my life,

To distract myself from the melancholy.
Tell me a story.
I've become the keeper of countless tales,
A vessel for anger, frustration, or despair.
While my own feelings stay well-veiled.
Ask me my story,
You'd be the first to do so.
When you discover my quiet struggle,
You'll wonder why no one knows.
Ask me my story,
And I'll tell you that i've kept it hidden.
For no one cared enough to ask,
And so I let their words become my prison.

35. Please

I used to say it without thinking,
A simple word, a fleeting sound.
A child's request, the magic word,

Before the weight of it was found.
Then it became a quiet whisper,
A prayer I hoped would keep you near.
No longer light, no longer harmless,
But laced with longing, filled with fear.
Yet it was never quite enough.
A thread too weak to pull you back,
You turned away, and in the dark,
The word went cold, the world went black.
Now it's just a ghost of echoes,
A syllable that turned to rust.
For once it fell from trembling lips,
And crumbled, lifeless, into dust.

36. To Find a Friend

to find a friend

with Gia

I walked alone through silent alleys,
A globe too dull, far and wide.

Trapped in empty lifeless valleys,
No voice to speak to, no hand to guide.
Then you appeared, a glow, a spark,
A light that cut through the gray.
Two drifting minds, now side by side,
No longer lost, no longer astray.
When you are low, I feel it too,
Like the chill of winter upon my skin,
But if you shiver, I'll stay close,
And share the warmth we've kept within.
And when you shine, I shine with you,
Like sunlight spilling gold and bright,
Through the dark and through the storm,
We'll chase the dawn and keep the light.

37. Blue

blue

Our planet is three fourths blue.
Which estimates to uncountable
Drops of water. Would you be able to

Drink all that, or is it impossible?
Now, think again. It may seem impossible,
But in reality, you have swallowed
Harder things before. You have gone through
Difficult times, your heart has been hollowed.
But still, you have triumphed
Over all the grief and sorrow.
You have striven every single day
To make a better tomorrow.
Hence, you come to the realization
That, to swallow the oceans of blue,
It is indeed possible,
As you will conquer this too.

38. Close Your Eyes

CLOSE YOUR EYES

We close our eyes when prayers rise,
With folded hands and wishes spun,
No vision guides the silent calls,

But faith endures like the burning sun.
We close our eyes when sorrow breaks,
When tears fall raw, heavy and free,
For sight can never hold the weight,
But darkness lets the soul breathe.
We close our eyes when dreams are made,
When longing paints the night in gold,
A world unseen, yet somehow near,
Where stories live, untouched, untold.
For all that's real is not in view,
Not bound by shape, sight, or art.
The truest things are never seen,
But only felt within the heart.

39. Glue

He was never whole to begin with,
Just shattered glass, a hollow frame.
A puzzle missing half its pieces,

A spark without a steady flame.
A false smile, a practiced answer,
Tied together, thread too thin.
But even stitches start unraveling,
When there's no one left to hold them in.
Then she arrived, out of nowhere,
A warmth that settled in his chest.
And where his seams began to falter,
Her laughter stitched them back to rest.
She was neither a bandage, nor a paper,
Nor a tape trying to hide the scars.
She was glue, tough and certain,
Holding all his shattered parts.

40. Joy

joy

I once found joy in the pages of books,
In songs that lingered past their end.
In city lights and passing faces,

In laughter pressed between the bends.
But slowly, the stories were rewritten,
My favorite songs suddenly seemed new.
The chords I followed, the dreams I chased,
Now all hold echoes, traced by you.
The life I built in quiet corners,
In the small joys and skies so wide,
Now finds its warmth, a steady rhythm,
With love that's always by my side.
So let the days stretch like verses,
Let time move slow or slip right through.
For every path I keep walking,
Somehow always leads back to you.

41. Kinds of Love

In the darkness, a candle glowed,
As he hunched over his scroll.
He tried to write his feelings down,

To bare the truth within his soul.
The words came, and slipped away,
Like water running through his hands.
He ran after the thoughts, but they dissolved,
Like footprints fading in the sands.
In truth, he didn't know how to express
The feelings that had caught him so deep.
Everything he wrote felt like an injustice,
To the love that he had sworn he would keep.
And then, a fleeting thought. "I knew two loves,"
"One you'd kill for, and one you'd die for."
"But you, you are different," he wrote.
"You are the love I'd live for."

42. Letting Go

letting go

They speak of closure like it's easy,
As if grief obeys the passing clock.
But some goodbyes still echo loudly,

Long after doors are closed and locked.
They always teach us how to free
The ghosts that haunt us in the night,
To let go is to stand alone,
To love what's gone, yet lose the fight.
Letting go is not erasing,
It's learning how to walk alone.
To carry love without its presence,
To build a house, but not a home.
Maybe time will not heal all wounds,
But it will teach the heart to bear,
The weight of love that once was there,
Soft as echoes, light as air.

43. Life-Changer

LIFE-
CHANGER

I used to watch the world on mute,
Counting days like tally marks.
A life that moved but never changed,

A sky that never held its sparks.
But then you came and changed it all,
Like dawn that melts the midnight air,
Suddenly, it all felt softer,
Like maybe hope was always there.
I used to see the end so clearly,
Like a fate I'd always known,
But now I flinch at every thought,
because I can't leave you alone.
For the first time, I fear the dark,
Not for me, but for your pain.
So I will stay, and see this through,
And walk with you through sun and rain.

44. Me and You

ME AND YOU

The sun sets your hair ablaze,
A warm shimmer in the midnight strands,
Your voice carries the warmth of sunlight,

Every word a melody, like magic in your hands.
In your presence, my mind awakens,
I notice every little thing you do,
I try to put it all in words,
But I know I'll never be enough for you.
For now, I'll settle for your quiet gaze,
And the calm you bring with every glance.
One day, I hope we won't need words,
Our hearts would simply take the chance.
In this world of change, you're my constant,
Through all the storms and skies so blue,
If I'm the writer, you'll be the words,
Because in this story, it's always me and you.

45. Unfinished

unfinished

Our song still plays, but fades too fast,
With echoes drifting out of tune.
We used to know each line by heart,

But now the words escape too soon.
This melody once wrapped around us,
A shroud of symphonies we swore would last,
But even harmonies cannot hold together,
When every note is from the past.
The chorus comes, but we stay quiet.
A fallacy we cannot mend.
The notes collapse in hollow echoes,
And every chord sounds like the end.
The final line is left unspoken,
The bridge undone, the ending wrong.
We mute the music of what we started,
And let go of our broken song.

46. Without You

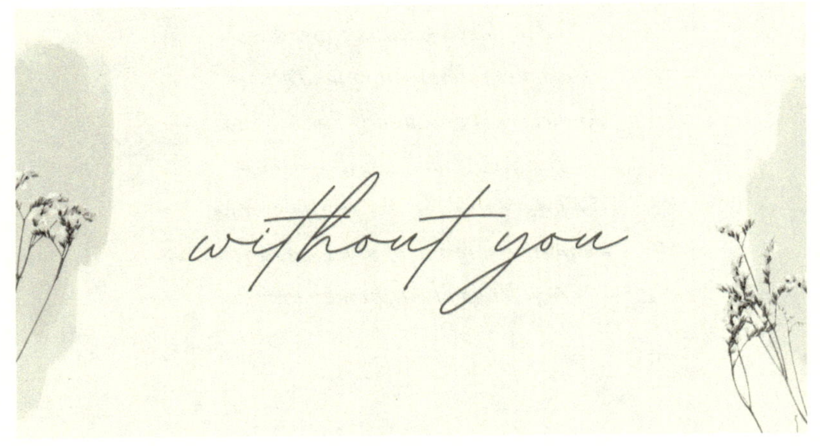

They tell me to keep walking forward,
That darkness thins, that pain won't last,
A promise of sun beyond the shadows,
A softer place, a brighter path.
You too, swore the night was not endless,
That even tunnels end in day.
Guiding me on, you promised I'd find it,
The golden glow to light my way.
But light alone could never save me,
Not if it shines and you're not there.
A hollow glow, a lacking heaven,

A warmth that quickly fades into air.
So, if the end holds any mercy,
If destiny be kind, if hope is true,
Then let the light stretch soft and golden,
And in its glow, a silhouette of you.

47. Wide Open

She knocked softly, spoke so sweet,
A warmth that felt like home, so free.
He let her in, he let her stay,

Too blind to see what she could be.
She made a home inside his heart,
Rewrote the words he used to say.
But he should've known a love like this,
Was just a storm that wouldn't stay.
The walls collapsed, the lights burned out,
She left, but left the wreck behind.
He stood among the shattered past,
And cursed himself for being blind.
She was like the fierce wind,
Destroying everything in her way.
But he had opened the window wide,
Had invited her in to stay.

48. You

you

You're the stars in every night,
You're the glow after the rain,
You're the dawn before the day,

You're the joy within the pain.
You're the spark in every storm,
You're the one helping me decide,
You're the glow of the distant horizon,
You're the one right by my side.
You're the fire burning bright,
You're the tide that pulls me near.
You're the truth I've come to know,
You're the voice I long to hear.
You're the light when hope feels gone,
You're the wish on every star.
You're the echo in all dreams,
You're home, no matter how far.

49. Coffee

coffee

with Viva Marie

My coffee spills and my pen goes dry,
A sigh is lost in empty air.

The clock ticks on but time feels stuck,
A day that goes on, but gets nowhere.
The mirror breaks, my keys are gone,
The sky turns gray without a sound.
Each step ahead feels like falling,
No solid ground, no way around.
I'm being ignored by most of my friends,
And there's no happy ending in my book.
It seems as if no one's there for me,
And I don't know where to turn or look.
But even storms must quiet down,
And darkness always yields to dawn.
The sky will clear, the ink will flow,
And the coffee stain will soon be gone.
I pour a new cup, and pull back the shades,
As I get a call back and time goes on,
Now the sunshine lights up my day,
And suddenly, not everything is going wrong.

50. Fullheart

fullheart

I finally have it.
Took the chance, just a fraction,
Turns out, it was scientific,

Third law, reaction.
I thought of not making it,
Of being merely the action.
I should've known that with my effort,
I'd get an outstanding reaction.
After all, the path was rough,
But giving up was never near.
I kept on moving, step by step,
And now the way ahead is clear.

A Playlist

As promised, here are some songs that directly or indirectly inspired some of the poetry in this book:

- Scott Street by Phoebe Bridgers
- Cool About It by boygenius
- Sweet Time by Porter Robinson
- Sidelines by Phoebe Bridgers
- champagne problems by Taylor Swift
- Image by Magdalena Bay
- Is There Really No Happiness? by Porter Robinson
- All The Stars by Kendrick Lamar & SZA
- Glue Song by beabadoobee
- Tied Together with A Smile by Taylor Swift
- closure by Taylor Swift
- Black Hole by boygenius
- Mirror by Porter Robinson
- Silence Between Songs by Madison Beer
- Easier to Love You by Porter Robinson
- Eita Tomar Gaan by Chandrabindoo

Once again, thank you for reading!

www.ingramcontent.com/pod-product-compliance
Lightning Source LLC
LaVergne TN
LVHW091026150826
845672LV00006BA/1706

* 9 7 9 8 8 9 7 4 4 3 4 3 7 *